Love Song to the Demon-Possessed Pigs of Gadara

Winner of the Iowa Poetry Prize

Love Song to the Demon-Possessed Pigs of Gadara

William Fargason

University of Iowa Press

IOWA CITY

University of Iowa Press, Iowa City 52242
Copyright © 2020 by William Fargason
www.uipress.uiowa.edu
Printed in the United States of America

Cover photograph © Devin Lunsford

Text design by Judy Gilats

Printed on acid-free paper

Library of Congress Cataloging-in-Publication Data
Names: Fargason, William, 1988– author.
Title: Love song to the demon-possessed pigs of Gadara / William Fargason.
Description: Iowa City: University of Iowa Press, [2020] | Series: Iowa
    poetry prize

Identifiers: LCCN 2019036803 (print) | LCCN 2019036804 (ebook) | ISBN
    9781609387051 (paperback) | ISBN 9781609387068 (ebook)
Subjects: LCGFT: Poetry.
Classification: LCC PS3606.A684 L68 2020 (print) | LCC PS3606.A684
    (ebook) | DDC 811/.6—dc23
LC record available at https://lccn.loc.gov/2019036803
LC ebook record available at https://lccn.loc.gov/2019036804

Epigraph on page vii is used with permission. *The Letters of Emily Dickinson*,
edited by Thomas H. Johnson, associate editor, Theodora Ward, Cambridge,
MA: Belknap Press of Harvard University Press. Copyright © 1958 by the
President and Fellows of Harvard College. Copyright © renewed 1986. Copyright © 1914, 1924, 1932, 1942 by Martha Dickinson Bianchi. Copyright ©
1952 by Alfred Leete Hampson. Copyright © 1960 by Mary L. Hampson.

Contents

and so I sing, as the Boy does by the Burying Ground—because I am afraid—
EMILY DICKINSON

I

When My Father Calls Me a Pussy

it means get up   it means he doesn't care
about the callous on my palm   or that I'm downwind
of the diesel fumes   it means swing harder   it means

I should feel   ashamed   that I stayed inside all day
playing my Game Boy   I should be proud of the mud
on my shins   kicked up by the four-wheeler

it means this gun   isn't going to shoot itself   it means
how does he tell everyone   in his Sunday School class
that his son wants to quit baseball   again

which means   he tried   failed   might as well be
a woman   it means I'm not the son   he wanted
I'm the son he got   it means when I gut

the deer   I should start at the nutsack   I should skin it
myself   with the guthook of the folding knife
I sharpened   it means this is what it means   to be

a man   and not   a wilted daisy   it means this is what
I think a man should be   which is to say   an ax
stuck in an oak tree stump   it means he loves

not me   but the version of me   I could be
which is to say   not me   which is   a stone
it means if I want to burn this thing down   I have to

3

start at the roots   I have to use   my own two hands
which can be knives held one way   feathers another
it means this is what my father   taught me

which is   to hate myself   it means his father
taught him not to cry   when he shaved his head
on the porch those summers   the hair sticking

to his forehead like grass clippings   it means
this is how   one man   cuts down another
in an effort   notch for notch   to grow larger

Polar Bear

I am standing on the edge of
a boat dock in Orange Beach,
Alabama, and I think of
the word: *polar bear*. Furthest thing
from here, but now the closest.
I have spoken it into being.
I think of all of it: of *paw*, of *fur*,
of *teeth*, of *fat* as insulation.
I think of all of nothing. Then I think of
all of polar bear and it's terrible.
Two or three boats go by—
a speeder with two women
(one, a red bathing suit, the other orange),
and a man driving. But I am with
polar bear, of all polar bear is,
and it, with me. I must put myself
into the arctic into the ice into the water.
I have a friend who has a
wintertime lake house, sauna,
gazebo overlooking a snowy creek,
and she told me how,
after sitting in the sauna for
an hour, she would go jump
into the frozen creek. The rush would
kill her. But I am nowhere near
snow. I am at the beach. Neon and car
horns from across the street, red
and green navigation lights of

boats reflecting off the water. I think
of the ice sculpture of a swan
in my condo lobby: how it melted
within hours, back into the form
it came from. How to get to a swan
out of ice, one has to chip away at
what it's not. But I am not
thinking of swan. Rather: polar bear.
I am thinking of all that is not polar bear
but should be. I must contain all
of polar bear, and all of polar bear
me. I just want to see it
the way it was meant to be seen.
I am standing here, at the end of
a boat dock, thinking of polar bear.
The dock's posts extend into
water, its posts covered in barnacles,
its posts looking almost like dirty white fur.
I am standing here at the end of
a boat dock thinking of polar bear
and of a sculpture of a polar bear,
but the ice (that I don't have) is melting.

My Father Feeding the Birds

You cut a hole through the screen
that covered your bedroom window
in that two-room farmhouse. You were six
or seven maybe, and would stick your wrist—
hand clasped around birdseed—out the hole
to feed the sparrows that darted about
in the Chinaberry tree. *Nurses*, you called them.
The cool night air pushed through the opening
until you were sure someone else must have felt
it inside. You knew what the birds knew:
that the sky was still blue even at night—
but no one could see it. You knew
they had eaten most of the fruit off
the tree, and came back each night
for your birdseed. And you knew to cover
the hole with the edge of the curtain to hide
what you were doing.
                    When you told me,
I didn't ask how you surely could hear
your parents one thin wall over;—or how
your father so drunk most nights he'd beat you
if he found out you spent half your lunch money
on birdseed;—or why your mother
and your two sisters would just sit there
never saying a word;—or how, when your thin arm
would reach further and further through that hole,
you'd get scrape marks so thin that your father
would believe you when you told him
it was from briars, just beyond the creek.

Love Song to the Demon-Possessed Pigs of Gadara

> *Then went the devils out of the man,*
> *and entered into the swine . . .*
> LUKE 8:33, KJV

Brave and grazing, the grass tread almost to dirt,
          you took on what was given to you.

Teach me to sleep, and I will teach you to swim.

The demons asked to leave
            the man—naked, shackled
                      then unshackled,
living in a sandstone cave outside of the city,

his long hair knotted and stringy, his torso and arms
          cut with stones he wouldn't unclench.

He begged only mercy, begged only to be left alone—
          but the Good Lord chooses who to save.

Maybe it's one of those stories:
                      you in the wrong place
at the wrong time, heroes only because you had to be.

Show me how to be blind, and I will show you how to resist.

          Just offshore of the Sea of Galilee, it was overcast—
the air humid, full of electricity.

The soft sound of your hooves pressing into dirt,
your hoofprints holy and blameless,

     —I swear, in the light,
you were beautiful there on the hillside
        becoming filled
with them, the whole of your bodies shaking.

Give me your courage, and I will give you my name.

The silence just before and just after,
and the black eyes as you leapt—
    no protest, no acceptance either.

You ran almost in unison,
      a dance without music,
   a curtain call,
and the crowd standing knowing this is what happens
once we find beauty:
     we must watch it leave.

Birthmark

When ducks come in to land on a lake,
they cup their wings inward to slow themselves
down. I told her that's what the birthmark

on the inside of her right thigh looked like.
A drake mallard. A wood duck. Its outline
against the sky at daybreak. She traced

my kneecap with her finger, said she was trying
to memorize every detail of me for when
we wouldn't see each other again. I didn't tell her

I was doing the same. My father used to take me
bird hunting, back before I moved away. Doves,
he said, flew different from the rest. They didn't

flap their wings quite as fast, or as frantic; they flew
more smoothly than finches or sparrows. He made
sure I aimed ahead of the target to make up for

the space the bird would fly once I pulled the trigger.
Leading the bird, he called it. Don't aim for where
the bird is, he said, aim for where the bird will be.

Fig Leaf

Another dream of you, fig leaf. The same almost
            every night: I'm naked. And cold.

Underbrush, thorn brambles, pine trees, hanging
moss, the mist of early morning
                streaming all the green veins.

Beneath the canopy, I lose my sense of direction.
        I thirst for no one,
fig leaf, but you. But you're too difficult to find.

Your branches don't bend like they used to.

        I take sinew and a bone needle,
sew you to you. But you don't hold together. You

never hold, and I have to start again:—
            here, the fig leaf;
                    here, the covering with the fig leaf.

The Lord made me naked but I don't want to be the way
            the Lord made me.

My eyes have been opened. I know good and evil and you
are good.
            For the first time in years, I'm ready to live
the rest of my life. But it has gotten harder to hide.

I'm bare and afraid. I need your covering, fig leaf.
　　　I need you to hold me,
as your branch held you,
　　　　　　forever in future tense.

Don't leave me alone with the Lord. Because
I can't take you with me. I'm awake.

I awoke. I still wake up each morning.
　　　Cold and afraid. Kicking off the sheets.

Floodwaters in South Carolina

Entering the water, the pastor—old, well-meaning—
made his way toward one of the caskets, his legs

below the water with the dead, his chest above
with the living, the entire family watching

from dry land as his hands slowly guided
the half-submerged box, ice in a glass, as it sailed

the new waters like a canoe, lilies still piled
on its lid, the pastor holding it gently in its second

baptism, as if he were taking the person's arm to his arm,
saying, *Hold this while I cover your mouth, while I push*

you under and pull you back up, in the name of the Father,
the Son, and the Holy Spirit. Reaching higher ground,

he tied off the casket's handle to a pole like a leash,
like an animal that could escape, run free. As if

we could tether the dead back in place—
here on earth, with us, for a little while longer.

Ash on the Tongue

Lord I will never have all the fruits of the spirit Lord
there is always one just out of reach when I was twelve

I asked my mother what exactly joy was but didn't

understand any words that came out of her mouth we were
in Yellowstone I would not leave the car again I was not

holy the sins of my young head each time I wanted to

look down a girl's shirt each curse word I thought but didn't
say fuck shit damn each thought sin each sin filled the backseat

like an animal I had to wrestle like the bear on the side

of the road I hung out the car window to take pictures of
the wind against my head gentle for once the fur I could almost

smell no more than eight feet away two boy body lengths

I could almost believe this closeness meant I was safe
the bear walked the cracked yellow line of the road my father

hours later pissed again I'm not having fun I should be

for how much money this cost him Lord my father stood
in the edge of the water a rainbow trout writhing between

his hands the camera flashed Lord if all light that is not you

is sin then how do I enjoy anything here there is no limit
to failure especially mine no limit to how many times

water can be frozen into snow then melted back

the water on the lodgepole pines as if it was still raining still still
I can see the lake like a window I want to roll down

the mountains the aspens in their yellow bloom

each leaf only tasted like ash on the tongue each winter
only made me want to palm the bark and recoil again

back into the belly of the ridgeline to be closer Lord to you

Cain

Cain in the ferns the underbrush the first
plant of its name my father named them all
Cain with a stone clenched in his hand
with a sharpened bone in his teeth Cain
of the soil hot underfoot Cain full of fruits
the Lord won't accept Cain I want to kill
my brother O Abel I want your blood
on my hands my hands covered in dirt the labor
I love Cain there are thorns in your voice
seeds unsown and put back in the hand Cain
whose chest is full of rocks whose veins are full
of noise Cain I ran three days followed
the moon followed the tree line down
to the edge of the ocean listened to the water
shape the land I kept running and found out
the world is too small I arrived back at Eve's feet
Cain there is no way to get away from
what you've done and the person who did it
Cain I am Cain and I am not Cain I am
the firstborn I deserve more than to work
the earth I remember my brother tending
the sheep before shearing time how delicate
he held their necks as he pulled the shearing blade
toward him how when he killed the lamb
the fat offering was flecked with blood
Cain I did what the Lord asked now where
is my reward my blessing Cain full of fear
full of corn no sweetness in his laughter

Cain as a child I found a snake made it my pet
built a fence around him in the grass with rocks
fed him crickets I found in the field when he
stopped eating I killed the crickets for him
dropped them in front of him tried frogs tried
birds even tried rats nothing worked Cain
when he died I used the fence rocks as a burial
mound as if what held him in in life could hold him
down in death as a child I didn't understand
how he could choose to stop eating just chose
to die Cain who watched every first animal
die Cain he who casts the first stone Cain I am
listening for your footsteps I am downwind
Cain if I tell the Lord I acted in anger I didn't
tell the Lord I had this planned Cain who yells
the name of his brother across the field Abel
whose name means breath whose body
could be expelled Cain who is my brother's
keeper Cain I will be the only descendant
of Adam until they replace Abel I want
what was promised my anger is my harvest
Cain do I have to answer the Lord do I
have to answer to anyone at all the wheat
doesn't call my name nor the corn the grapes
the apple trees Cain why art thou wroth Cain
who could kill his brother in his sleep
who could do it painlessly but wants to see
the life leave Abel the bastard I want to watch
him bleed out like the season's first rain
I want to watch him I will make his body
an offering I did this for you Lord and this

17

is how you repay me I inherit nothing
but dust Cain whose callous hands still hold
the stone whose fingernails are caked in dirt
like five black crescent moons Cain who
tries to turn the stone against himself Cain suicide
has not been invented yet Cain if I could hurt
myself I would but even the Lord left a mark
on me so no man could harm me not even myself
Cain sin was at my door I invited him in gave him
some of my dinner now I hear only my brother's
voice every time the Lord speaks Cain my brother
below the Lord above I will I can set things
right Abel stood in my way of the Lord I will
ask the Lord's forgiveness knowing there is no
Abel left to forgive me only myself only Cain
there is no escape from the self my brother

Emo, 2005

Testing out your sister's Clinique eyeliner,
never sure of how thick to make the black
beneath our eyes, then blacking out
our fingernails with a Sharpie that would wear
first at the edges from the sweat, me pulling

up a pair of jeans your girlfriend let me
borrow before skinny jeans for men existed,
were even a thing yet, and you in the mirror
flat-ironing your choppy boy bangs. How ridiculous
we looked, this weekly preshow ritual of belonging,

before riding downtown in your blue Ford Ranger
to see whichever band it was that week, before
the doors opened at seven. And that was the fall
we saw My Chem play, and I had planned to
do it then, but wanted to see them play first, then

hang myself from my parents' porch with a note
stapled to my chest like a boy sent to the store
with his mother's list pinned to his shirt. But here
we were, seventeen, more pissed than we knew
what to do with, lost in the sweat of the crowd

and the noise of the music, thankful
for the distortion, that wall of sound, trapped
almost by the sheer number of bodies
on every side, but grateful for once not to
have to make a decision about which way to go.

Not an Entrance

Leaving St. Vincent's Mental Health
Outpatient Wing you have to walk through
emergency care, through with the day,
the first week of therapy that you signed up for
not so willingly is done, so you walk down
the hall to the door that leads outside
shrouded in a too-white light, the sliding door
next to the manual door, the one marked
not an entrance, as if you wanted to go back in,
another session, another pill to try, another
week of this shit, the marked door not

an entrance but a porthole, a peephole, a bored-out
deadbolt, a credit card slid through the crack
in the door, the light from the other side
like a knife in your eye, a thief tied to a kite,
the boat that dredges the river not just
for your body, but any body, just in case,
maybe if we make just one more pass
the dredging hook will catch, and we can leave
this eternal lake, have proof of an exit,
the drowned boy, his purpled skin, who looks
like you but is not you, not him, not her,
not an entrance but a fireplace lined with soot
ten years thick, the taste of salt water
against your gums, stuck between your teeth,
a kind of meat, your own flesh, not a door
but a window, the body, there you are, standing

in her apartment lobby with your fists dug
as deep as your pockets will allow, knowing
what is in front of you could be anything
but the tires hydroplaning after the e-brake
is pulled, a story not about the sun, not about
the moon either, but about knots untied,
the hinges of your hands in the half-light,
the Get Out of Jail Free card, the only reason
you played the game in the first place, to find
a way back, the only trail home, the lost map
you kept in the glovebox of the car beneath
all the receipts piled up like a tiny snow-covered
mountain range, the map that no one needs
until they do, until you're stuck like that time
you yelled fuck into the wind as the wind
filled you on that interstate shoulder, the steam
surrounded you like a beast from a swamp,
the road itself not an entrance but an exit, a respite,
something that has felt too familiar for too long,
like waking up, which is not an entrance, not
even a chamber or a holster but the spiral of the rifling
in the barrel, like a strand of DNA or a pool
of water down a drain, which is neither entrance
nor exit but a point of transfer, the battery
sparks back when you tap the wrong clamp
to its terminal like fireworks celebrating
the failure of your life, what you felt for so long
wasn't right, the sparks saying you fool, you knew
all along that this wasn't an exit but you
kept trying anyway, you desired every entrance
to be an exit, like the bike wheel left chained

to the lock after the thief took everything
else and only left you that one wheel, which is not
any way to get anywhere, but here, in front
of a door that reads *not an entrance*,
which could be the definition of each day
you can't stand to begin, that daily disappointment
of waking up to an entrance, that same self,
those pill bottles lining the bathroom shelf
like an audience who watches you like the entrance
you have been and will become, groggy and trying
to remember which bottle is the entrance
and which one the exit, so you take it, wanting
to arrive at any other shoreline but this one,
this same sun, this morning you didn't ask for,
this snot clogging your nose, the cat mewing
at the bedroom door because she's hungry,
the cold floor you sit on, the ash of your eyes
you rub to ignite, just wanting any kind
of light, the trash can overflowing with
crumpled paper from every unsent letter
that felt like an entrance but proved only
to be an exit, when all you really wanted to say was
can I just quit yet, into that exit, death,
that final knowledge, can I just push the door
hard enough that even the exit becomes
an entrance, not an entrance but an exit.

II

Nudes

We must've been standing next to the rock
climbing wall of our church youth group center
when she asked me if I'd ever seen a vagina,

and I said of course, because my parents
had the internet, and so she took
my phone—which had a camera, which was

still a new feature then—and said
I bet you don't even know what one looks
like, then went to the bathroom, my phone

in her hand. I stood next to that thirty-foot
wall of fake rock for what must
have been close to ten minutes, each handhold

bright against the grey: alien green humerus
bone socket, red apple the size of my hand,
the beginner's two-hand hold only six feet

off the ground like a yellow moon
you could climb to reach, and I did, so many
afternoons my mother would drop me off

for a fistful of hours, and I would put on
that crotch-tight harness one leg
at a time, click the carabineer to my waist

and up I went. I was a god up there, I could
see the sum of my kingdom, I was
what I wanted to be. In my sixteen-year-old

mind everyone else there was watching me
each time I barely made it to the last
purple handhold then slapped the top

of the wall to show I'd conquered gravity,
the enormity of the wall proving itself
no more than three inches thick,

supported by a skeleton of steel beams.
But she was back from the bathroom, said
here, I told you, the phone flipped open

and I could see the other side,
the temple curtain torn, and I stared
at that skyline turned on its axis, I was,

in that moment, a teenaged astronaut
untethered, holding the holy picture
she gave to prove me wrong, to prove

life does exist on other planets,
the universe rendered in 1.2 megapixels,
the glow of the screen, the peach

of her skin so grainy all I could make out
was what it was not, a smile
she gave me as she walked away.

Carving

Before the cancer, my grandfather would sit
in his converted-garage workshop after supper
with a block of pine the size of my forearm,

and whittle away at it, a carving knife resting
flush in his palm, pulling the blade back to him
in long smooth motions. When he switched knives

to start the features, he would take a sip of bourbon
from a BAMA jam jar, its purple flowers almost
completely scuffed off. Each block slimmed down

into an outline, an outline into a figure, a figure into
a person. These imitations of German woodcarvings,
these caricatures, really: a woman in a blue dress,

her exaggerated breasts; a man in unhinged overalls,
bulbous nose and gaping mouth stained and painted
in crude reds and yellows. They smelled fresh as

death, as far as I remember: the sap of a felled tree,
the chemical flush of wood stain. *Little uglies*,
he called them. He preferred soft wood—

basswood or white pine—something that would do
what he wanted it to do: to take the knife
as blessing, to accept the prayer he pissed away at.

My Father's College Roommate

Auburn, 1978

He would watch my father from across
their dorm room, each step and turn made, the outline
of each leg and curve. After a tough workout,

my father would peel off his sweat-soaked gym shorts
and shower in their tiny dorm shower, so close
to their bedroom that the steam would cloud

the light fixture on the ceiling. My father would
emerge, towel draped in all the right places,
half-dry, water beaded on his taut skin. How young

he must have looked, a colt penned in a stall.
Sore, my father would ask his roommate to rub a knot
in his back, loosen the muscles. This should have been

a scene in an old romance film, slow pan
from him to him, but it isn't. There should be
a kind of cello suite playing softly. But there isn't

and never was. My father didn't know his roommate
liked to touch him—so when his roommate paused
in his massage for a second too long, laid his head

on my father's back, my father jumped up, clocked
him in the jaw, sent his body to the floor. In his
confusion my father lashed out—scared at what

he didn't know, he had never been shown tenderness
before. The sound must have been soft, as touch
can be, a kiss or a handshake or a fist in the teeth.

Notes on Bridge Burning

Make sure to point out her flaws.
Character flaws cut deepest. How she can't
commit to a favorite ice cream flavor,
let alone you. Point out inconsistencies
in her speech, when she says untrue things
just to hurt you. It won't be that you can't
believe her, but you never could trust
someone who loved you. She loved you?
When you find Billie Holiday lyrics scribbled
in the back of the Faulkner book she borrowed,
don't let the melody get stuck in your head.
Make sure to betray the secrets she told you
in confidence. Maybe the one about how
each night she had to turn the TV to a static
channel, then cover the screen with a shirt
so she could fall asleep to the white noise.
Tell her friends. Invent a rumor about her
cheating on her new boyfriend with you,
and then deny ever starting anything. End
everything by turning her words against her.
How is this selfish—my wanting space—
when you're the one who left? Use short
declarative sentences. They're most effective.
If she calls to tell you you left your red cardigan
at her place, tell her she can keep it. She can
give it away. Tell her you loved that sweater,
but burn it, give it to the squirrels. Remind
yourself: she was too tall; and you're too

unstable. When you run into her in public,
look at her as if she bombed a hospital,
or look straight through her, as if she existed
like a window. When you meet her new boyfriend,
smile at the way he looks like he could be
your younger brother. The same stupid haircut
and the same stupid boyish love-glaze plastered
on his face that you had a few months before.
The same empty longing in his eyes, like swimming pools
drained in winter, staring back at you like
a mirror. The same futile need to control
the conversation. He won't shut up. Maybe
you should shut up. Or maybe for once,
this time, you shouldn't. When you start to
miss her, miss her. Tell her *fuck off* can,
in fact, be a mature way to end a conversation.
No it can't. Change her name in your phone
to DO NOT ANSWER. Don't feel too bad.
That's what she would want and this is
not about what she wants anymore. Tell her
she is and was and continues to be a mistake,
a wrong number, a lost library card, a credit card
being run up in San Francisco and Tennessee.
Always have the last word. Never take back
anything. Never give anything away.

Sour Wine

I didn't want to believe the Lord
when he told me I wasn't
guilty anymore. Because I knew
better: I was there. I saw
the need for the blood. I was

the sponge soaked with sour wine
—raised on a hyssop stalk, pressed
against the Lord's lips—to make
him feel the need: the purpose

for his death, my death through
his death, or how I'd already died
a hundred times before, back into
that stilted rebirth.
                    The French
call the orgasm *la petite mort*,
or *little death*, right?

But all our sins have been annulled,
have been covered by the guilt—
its weight necessary, its poplar
yoke wore my shoulders raw.

I've felt the guilt grip me more
passionately than I've ever felt
the love hold me. All the barley seeds
I scattered among briers—
but my burden of conviction
must be equal.

                    Guilt is the love
I've been given from the Lord.
Therefore, I've loved,
and love.

                  Some days I feel
you've never left me.

Upon Receiving My Inheritance

I said Thank You father for giving me
this disease that will one day bind my bones
together at each joint Thank You genetics
for passing this down to me and not my sister
perfectly healthy Thank You for choosing
me Thank You bones some days I can't sit up
without crying some days I can't sit up at all
Thank You painkillers for your blessed strength
when I have none help me not feel Thank
You doctors and doctors and doctors and every
room I waited in for you I still wait now Thank You
mother for your company every room is less
empty because of you Thank You father for all
the years you had this disease undiagnosed blamed it
on lifting lumber or the years of football
father you must have felt the same pain but didn't
have the words for it yet didn't know how to
voice pain except with your hands except to ask
more of me at the table scribbling my homework
with a dull pencil Thank You father my heart
has a tattoo of a heart with barbed wire wrapped
around it Thank You body I left myself came back
and realized I was still there all along Thank You
mirror the body is always more reliable
than the mind Thank You hands I can still form
into fists underneath the sheets Thank You
doctors for telling me that if my bones fuse
I will be like a tree Thank You for that metaphor

Thank You for the images of Dante's forest
infested with harpies Thank You river water
fir trees open air I have tasted your sweetness
and turned away Thank You trees for your resistance
in every thunderstorm that passes outside
my window I wake up and still see the oak tree
standing Thank You rain I can only hope
to add rings beneath the bark I can only
hope to one day be cut down and counted

Second Life

In a past life my wife / was Bathsheba, / but I wasn't / David, or even Uriah. I was / me. I guess I hadn't had / a second life / yet. She goes on / about this over beers, about her past self, as if / opening a knife in one hand, / eyeing the blade, turning / it over in her palm. / When she gets up, turns around, / I can see her / black underwear / through a rip in her jeans. / She says / she knew David was watching / her, she / liked to be watched, still does, / says David was too rough in the sack, / finished too quick, didn't pay / attention to her after. Typical / of a man, she says, / ordering two more beers. It's true / or it isn't, it doesn't make much / difference. The things you learn about / someone after / you think you've learned all / you can—you can't. / That was the year I went sober, / the year that everything / that could get stuck / in my eye did. / It's not like I killed anyone, / she says. Not really.

Watching My Father Pray over the Lord's Supper

This was the first time I had seen
my father in a state where anyone could have

sucker punched him or stolen his wallet.
Head bent, he sat next to me in the pew,
his arms stiff marble columns. He cradled

the small cup of grape juice in his left hand
with four of his fingers, the cup itself

like a shot glass ready to be tipped up.
And in his right, he pinched the tiny cracker,
the body of Christ. I couldn't have been

more than ten, watching him only
because his eyes were closed, my own

hands empty. My eyes went from him
back to the awful red carpet below,
not even the right shade of blood,

the pattern of orange triangles overlaid
with a tan square, the pattern repeating

as I darted my eyes from one square
to the next, my head still bowed like his.
The piano sounded far away, each note

slowed to half-time, as if I were
thinking the music, replaying a song

I once knew. Even then I thought I could have
overpowered him in that moment,
I could have killed him for all the times

I thought he was going to kill me,
like the time he pulled me out of bed

by my shirt neck, broke a ruler, a vase,
a picture frame to prove a point, then started
crying in his anger, his arms shaking.

I could have spilled real blood. I wanted to.
But anyone could've mistaken his quiet

for thought, or hunch for reverence,
and they would've been part right.
When the preacher, who I had forgotten

was even up there, read *This is my body,
do this in remembrance of me*, my father

ate the cracker, and when the preacher
said *This is my blood, which is poured out
for you*, my father's head tipped back,

eyes open, draining the tiny cup.
He let me hold it after he finished,

and I held it up to the light, my father's
lip print on the plastic, a sort of terrible
kindness I wanted, but was never

given, not without a sacrifice
that even then I knew I could never give.

Elegy with Digital Flowers

I am searching for myself, clicking on link
          after link, and one website asks me to leave
a digital flower below the image of my great-

          grandfather's grave, loading line by line on the screen
like a song. I have never visited his grave, never knew

          him, and this is the closest I've been. The pines
that surround the plot look older than I am. There's
          a close-up image of the tombstone, its grey

like static on TV. The zoomed-out photo reveals
          a carved line down the middle of the stone, an arrow

below the last name, his wife's name on the other
          side. I can leave daffodils, yellow pixelated edges,
tulips, pansies, or a "realistic" rose, which looks less

          like a rose and more like a woman dancing, green petal
of her skirt, white petals of her arms extended. I leave

          nothing, take nothing, want real flowers, real dirt,
the rawness of a shovel hilt in my hand, but I keep
          clicking anyway. On the top of the tombstone: two hands

shaking, but no bodies, the arms disappearing back into
          the stone. All I'm left with is hands locked

in a forever-embrace, a greeting or a farewell,
     an impression with no body to ground it. And in the last
photo's background, the front bumper of a Jeep, tires

     edging in, as if whoever took these photos had a way
to enter the graveyard and a way to leave.

When My Father Tells Me
My Great-Grandfather Was in the KKK

he tells me in a hushed voice   as if someone could
overhear him   as if those sins could come back

into that living room   lined with animal heads

and gun cabinets   a fallow deer   a mountain goat
two largemouth bass   a red fox at full alert   listening in

he leans in when he tells me   as if anything could change

where we are   no one can change   where they are
only where they are going   we share a family name

my father   my grandfather   my great-grandfather

I'm the fourth   and the last   of that lineage
that system of blood   my father's hand

runs through   the dense fur of the moose head

on the wall   he says one day   all of this will be mine
it makes sense now   why he said for me to always keep

the pistol he gave me   in my glovebox   when driving

through a   bad   part of town   what he meant was
a   black   part of town   I remember as a kid

driving with him   to his hunting club in a small town

south of Selma   we stopped for gas   my father's tense
shoulders as he left me alone   he showed me where

his snubnose .357 was   in the center console   *just in case*

I was taught to be afraid   I grew up being told
to shoot   at the first sign of movement

no matter the fog in the woods   I left that state

with more than a century of sins inherited   the pine trees
in my backyard no longer innocent   the very grass

sang everything I didn't know   I knew was wrong   I must be

different   I can't let what I was taught   be what I teach
if I leave this place   or don't   I carry those pines

those sins   in me   like sod carries the soil it was cut from

Sugar

The summer my father swallowed bees
the honeysuckle outside our house bloomed

longer, larger even than usual. In the heat of June,
he pushed the mower back and forth,

always matching the lines the wheels made
in the grass to the edge of the next row

as he came back, his dirty white t-shirt draping
only where it wasn't stuck to the sweat, his arms

powdered with clippings. My father wiping his
brow. My father saying the varmints are back at it again.

My father saying we could use the rain,
saying I should go outside more.

My father saying a lot of things. As he
worked, he left his open can of sweet tea

on the porch railing. Sugar is sugar to any insect.
He took a break for a drink, didn't stop

until the can was empty. Later, he said
he could feel them inside stinging all the way down.

Anchor

father saying pull in the anchor we must leave soon the storm
coming in faster than we expected will beach us if I don't pull it in

faster father jumping into the water starboard side to help
the two women whose boat had already struck the shore

I pull up the chain the weight of it my arms no thicker
than the metal braid they hold but again jellyfish season

those water ghosts stuck to the chain I grab their tentacles
unseen the burning but I must pull faster pull harder my hands

covered in welts I am a man I am a man I am a boy the clouds
dark and getting darker fast father will be back any minute I will

be ready when he returns I will let us leave I will take us home

III

Nocturne for a Red Fox

Leaving your house last night for the last time
I saw a red fox on the side of the road, fur matted,

wet eyes glaring through the waist-high grass

off East Adelphi—so quick I thought I'd imagined it.
Did I imagine it? I knew its presence had to mean

something, I wanted it to. I wanted to

believe in it, in what you said, how goodbye
was just see-you-soon,—you so earnest

with your constant eye contact, fixed as if I were

a passing car you wanted to step in front of.
Not everything has to be sadness. Not every

goodbye a hymn. This is how I convince myself,

turning off the light, with early August outside
waiting for me to walk into its arms, like a lock, opening.

Images of Kurt Cobain's Shotgun Released

The rust that covered the chamber
was the first thing I noticed,
the chamber open as an empty tomb,

as someone who could just walk away,
a shadow at midday, hammer pulled back.
April, almost twenty-two years ago:

the last time the gun held a bullet you held
the gun like the door that it was. Some nights
before I got blackout drunk I would hide

the hollow-point bullets to the Colt .357
my father gave me for graduation,
its silver smile. I did not want the gun

so easy, so ready. The engraving
on both sides of your shotgun, so delicate
it could've been carved with the end

of a snapped guitar string: a duck,
wings beating against the water, trying
to take off. A pheasant in the grass

at full stride. Both animals forever
fleeing, like a song stuck on repeat
that keeps starting over again.

When You Were out of Town Last Weekend

I pressed my ear against every window
in the house. I named the horse Peanut.
I rode the horse alone. Every bank of snow

had your face in it. The tree branches
only offered dead fruit, but I ate it anyway,
branch and all. Here I hungered for

distance, but what I found instead was
muddy paths with tracks I couldn't
identify. The only sweat I tasted

was my own. No wind blew
in this place, or if it did, I couldn't
feel it. When I grew tired of riding, I walked

beside Peanut. The world seemed almost
post-apocalyptic without you in it.
With every step the hardwood floors

sang to me, the fir trees beaded
with my breath. The moss pointed
toward north even though I didn't want

to know. Even though I knew where
I was heading without you was
directionless, was full of frost. Summer,

winter, summer again, you were gone
too long, each ice melt left me alone
in a doorway or head tilted down

to drink the cold river water. I heard
my own voice echo back when I found
a cave three body-widths deep. How strange,

to find myself in the shallows. These trails
I'd cut other weekends alone, the grass
matted and ground bare. Here I hunted only

myself, which took me to wheat fields
my legs could disappear into. With a fistful
of dirt, I filled my mouth and waited for rain.

Nocturne with Choking in Calloway Gardens

The quickest way to death
is choking   this is my fear
not death but the choking
I have felt recently like something's
stuck in my throat   the moon perhaps
a cloud passing   an iris dilated
The garden is quiet this time
of night   No water bubbling
in the fountain   no fountain
just a gravel path I follow
Each azalea blossom bud I pluck
and squeeze in my palm
feels like feeling in control of something
for once   even if nature always
has the final say   even if each clasp
pulls apart so easily   the petals
sheathed in green   Each one I pick
says there's a whole acre more
waiting   My grandmother once
turned red then blue   a piece
of meat lodged in her throat   My throat
is lined with rings like a cat's
I often seize up over simple things
bread or kudzu   Now at the dinner table
I want to say   Excuse me I need to leave
for I have already swallowed enough
darkness enough enough   Man cannot
live on   Man cannot live

on alone   There is not a difference
in a root in my vein or one in my head
the branch ends up in the same place
Little fist of daisies   how small
your petals   you will die soon
with no root left to hold you
The past is   but the past is   but the dirt
under my fingernails   I have dug
a trench around myself   Now I am
protected three feet in all
directions   but also stuck in place
I have forgotten the taste
of blackberries or okra   stained tongue
or salt   the smaller things
I never had a choice
of what I ate   I ate it anyway
a good child is silent   a good child
doesn't sing   there is pine sap
on my palms   the garden is full
too full   even without me   Hope is
a burden I gave up long ago
I no longer wait for spring
or much of anything   no hot water
boiling for tea   no phone call
no hand on my hand to remind me
I'm not walking alone   My head is
crumbling in on itself   If death is actually
sleep then I have been so very tired
for so very long   twenty years
to be exact   I am afraid I want

to eat every flower in the garden
until I can't breathe anything
but the sweetness   My therapist
is convinced I'm not a threat
to myself   that makes one of us

Aquarium

You want to keep feeding the fish
inside you, but you keep

eating the fish because you're hungry.
This is not the way it should go.

No one said you would not be hungry.
You knew the dimensions of the aquarium

inside you, knew it was inside you.
She who fogged the glass didn't know

that you'd eaten the fish, but you did and do.
You hear the aquarium inside your chest

crack, and before you know it, the carpet
is soaked with bleached coral,

plastic kelp, and multi-colored gravel.
This is not the way it should go.

This is not how anyone should go under—
the water you contained now contains you.

Tightrope

On the TV, a man is attempting
to cross the Grand Canyon by walking
on a tightrope. He holds
a large pole to balance himself,
slippered feet cupped around
the two-inch metal wire. What poise,
balance. We are watching this together
because you've driven over
to pick me up for dinner, but neither
of us will turn off the TV
or stand up. By now, we are invested
in the outcome. You pull closer

to me on the couch. Will he make it
across? Will the cameras keep rolling
if not? His family waits on the other
side of the canyon. Your hand
on my leg tightens when the wind
picks up, causes the man to bend
down, pivot the pole to regain balance.
I can smell the perfume you're wearing
because we are going to a nice place
for once, that French restaurant
with all the candles. Your neck smells of lilacs,
or pancakes burning. I can never tell.

I know you won't leave him
for me—and the man is halfway across
by now, the wind pushing against him,
forcing him to pause again—but I can
hope. I kiss your cheek. You smile.
Ten minutes of him moving one foot
at a time, holding his weight
against the wire, 1,500 feet up
in the air, no safety net. You ask if
your car will be towed if you parked on
the street. I don't think so. But we have
to leave for our reservation, we are
going to be late. I turn off the TV.
Looking back, how terrible
it might have been if you loved me.

Seeds as Nails

You are in love with the medicated
version of me, which is to say,
me. Each time I don't tell you why

I'm actually upset, I drive a nail
into the wall. Before long, I will
have so many nails in the sheetrock

I can barely fall against it without
cutting my face. What I can't feel
can't hurt me, I suppose. I don't want

to hold resentment like a seed inside
me, growing with each secret I don't
tell you. What you don't know

can't hurt you. Come pull each nail up
and curl next to me in the bed. I want
to fuck for so long and so hard that you forget

where I came from, who I am.
We're building something, after all.

Porcelain Nocturne

Here, it always rains. No matter. We share an umbrella,
the branches of a tree, the light from the moon. Imagine

the moon as a tiger. This doesn't change the moon.

No matter. She is glazed ceramic. No matter. I trust
her hands in the clay. She pulls a tiger from the kiln,

still hot. The moon was never, can never be a tiger,

no matter how long our hands work. Imagine the moon
as clay. The moon is clay. No longer alone, we mold

each other again into night. We add another stripe to the tiger.

Ode to the Mattress on the Side of the Interstate

Broken and waving, I catch you barely
        out of the corner of my passing window,
                sitting there under the overpass, fallen out
        of a truck like common trash. Your broken
back arched over the guardrail, your open cavity
        torn at the side like Christ, like a woman's

                shawl unpinned blowing in the hot air.
        How many secret nights are you spilling
out? Whose nights are they now? I'm tired
        as hell from another night where I wake up
                sweating, but I have to keep driving past
        you in the edge of the waist-high grass,

the overgrown kudzu, all but forgotten.
        You can no longer provide a safe night
                to anyone, you are nothing anyone craves.
        I want to pick you up, strap you to the roof
and keep driving, I could find another bed,
        a bigger bed, for you to rest on, we could sleep

                so long we forget what day it is. I can,
        I could try to find us both a home—away
from the cold wind of passing cars, any home
        warm and sweet—but am I too many miles away
                from you now, too far to turn back? Would I even
        remember where you are, which mile marker?

The Day

your breath left with such thunder
I felt the earth in that cold ICU room
hold me in a new gravity

the flatlined noise fading out
as if underwater the nurses at the doors
of my chest the hands I pushed

into my pockets didn't feel like
my own nothing anymore felt
my own but there you were little

heap little body under a bed sheet
nothing more you were meant to inherit
the earth you were meant to pull through

now I am left without a father
trying to fill my palms with water

There Is No Power in Blame

so I blame the water for freezing I blame
my breath for the clouds in front
of my face fogging my glasses I keep
wiping them off but the steam's relentless
I blame the heat for every beauty
it undoes the rocks the fire the frost I blame
the cracks in the ice for forming so soon
this year their lines a language I can't read
yet I blame the honeysuckle for its smell
for it's inviting so I want to cross
the creek I blame the knot for coming untied
for causing me to stumble into the edge
of the water the legs of my pants stuck
wet like a second skin I blame the leaves
for their inaccuracy for never fully covering
me I blame the windowpane for busting
under the pressure of my two hands
why is it so weak I thought it could hold me
I blame the light through the blinds for never
being enough to wake me up I'm late
I'd be late again if I ever tried to make it
on time I yell to no one in the dream where
I'm late but still asleep how many nights
do I blame for curtains of grass blades I drug
across my face for always being most afraid
when first awake I blame the sweaty sheets
the overgrown weeds of my beard I blame
the caffeine for keeping me awake

I blame the thorn for the prick the prick
for the blood I blame my tongue for not
minding the taste I blame my shirt for ripping
when my father pulled me out of bed
asleep and said you embarrassed me
son do you know how I hate embarrassment
do you know how I hate I blame not my father
but his father no his father's father I blame
the booze for the man that man turned into
my father's face a blurred fury red
eyes full of almost-tears from almost
saying what he has for so long never said
I blame my mother for nothing nothing
but staying silent I blame my watch for never
counting my breaths or the space I hold between
them a trick my therapist taught me once
when I told her I too often lost my pulse
in thought or in fear and called an ambulance
one too many times so now I blame my watch
my dumb watch for not stopping when I say
stop for not keeping track of the now
the now the tick louder than her words
the clock of her mouth I blame the cigarettes
for the cough for never letting me stay full
of smoke never letting me ascend any higher
than the red chipped paint on this park bench
I blame the valves of my heart for the flick
and stutter the reason I check my pulse
to find my center to hear the proof I'm
still alive as when I release the safety
of my father's 30.06 my cheek against the stock

trying to remember to let the kick surprise
me that's how I will know I made a clean
shot I blame the deer for standing in front
of my gun I blame my hand for pulling
the trigger for always sinning without me
knowing I blame every sermon
for making sin sound musical like a music
I could hear in the next room maybe Bach
maybe not I blame the sin for the guilt
I blame it again but am I guilty of
everything that gives me guilt or how do I
get away from my conscience for one
goddamn minute I blame my conscience
for the overflowing wastebasket of hate
I made of myself I would've thought at this age
I would like myself more that I would be
okay with being alive because every day
I blame my eyes for waking me up I blame
the kitchen for getting my order wrong
even though I mumbled to the waitress I still want
my toast with my eggs is there really a point
to eating most days I blame my fucked heart
for being what it is because I did not ask
for termites in the walls but then again
no one ever does I blame my grandmother's
ring I inherited for being too small the ring
is a six and a quarter but she wears a six
and a half I blame the wheel bearings
for busting blame the rusted sway bar
for the noise that sounds like cardinals
with every bump I hit I blame the axle

for holding the wheels on in the first place
blame the whole damn car for staying on the road
every time I wanted to jerk the wheel
when crossing a bridge I blame the water oak
growing in my gutter its tiny sprout above
the rim of my roof because love is not often
enough I blame every pocket for the holes
it gets blame the holes for lost house keys
I blame the window for being too small
for me to fit through my body is always
halfway between two places it would be
just as easy to drift toward death
as it would be to try to feel alive again
to open the house door for once and feel
the air-conditioning from the twenty-year-old
window unit rattling its song every hour
I wait for its return I blame gravity
for holding me to this balcony I blame
the height the drop for looking so inviting
why am I not taller maybe if I was taller
I would have one less thing to blame she is
taller than me her nipples almost staring me
in the eyes when she wears those heels I feel
shorter even than normal the year I fell off
the growth curve was the same year my mother
forgot to take me to the doctor for my yearly
check-up I blame the calendar for that for
every day stuck in a box on a page with no
choice left for me but to cross it out this date
with her I'm late for I wore my good shoes
she descends blameless beautiful I said

I wouldn't let her height bother me I wouldn't
blame her I wouldn't so instead I blame
the fence for being too close to the tree
I blame the tree for growing around the fencepost
until they are one I have to rip these posts
out one by one it's the only way to the other
side of the field the clump of earth each post
takes with it leaves a hole the size of my head could be
a grave for just my head I built the fence I blame
the fence I built the tree I blame the tree
I planted the tree I should blame me I blame me

IV

The View through My Father's Scope Is a Planet

full of short sage   two whitetail bedded
near where   the equator would be   the blackness
around the scope's light   is empty space   the red dirt
or brush   toward the south   has patches of grass
continents or islands   the whole land mass covered
in a haze   that could be from the sunlight off
the barrel   I can almost forget   the crosshairs are not
a compass   can almost forget   they don't divide
the planet into   four hemispheres   my father's eye
his hands around the stock   polished maple or cherry

every time   he scolded me   for not pulling
the trigger right   I closed my eyes   the shot should
take me by surprise   the sphere unlit   should collapse
into a black hole   my father's voice   the voice
of my creator   his voice over the gunshot's ring

I wasn't proud of what I'd done   he was   what had I
done   the pines across the clearcut   the mud
on my boots   I reshaped the landscape   with a bullet
I tried to prop   the body up   against a thicket
of underbrush   I tried to push the tongue
back in its jaw   for the pictures   I tried to leave
the field of alfalfa   the woods followed me

Song

I have seen the kingdom in the backyard
behind a group of four oaks, wooden planks
joining each to each. A shelter. I have
seen the kingdom, and it is a hermit thrush
with a piece of popcorn too big for its beak.
I have seen the kingdom in her eyes
over and over becoming and unbecoming
a kingdom, a neighborhood, a safe camp,
or a city, a town, each brick and steel beam
lowered into place. With a fresh pane,
I have seen the kingdom, the kingdom
of not *only* but *also*, the purr of water
in the kitchen basin not cleaning anything
but offering it anyway. Kissing her wrists
is a form of prayer, but who am I
even praying to when I am standing outside
the kingdom, looking in the windows covered
with ice and dead ivy, fogging the glass
with my breath? I have seen the kingdom
love-hungry, love-dry, the soft sound
of my bare feet in the grass. I have seen
the kingdom but failed to annotate it
with footnotes made from palm fronds—beached
on the kingdom I learned to swim with my eyes
closed, learned to float face-up in the sun.
The kingdom in each cracked line of her
palm: Ursula Minor; Canis Major; the belt
of Orion; Regulus and Denebola forming a lion,

Leo—the kingdom of yesterday arriving
as the light of today. The kingdom of her
standing naked in the kitchen cutting
a peach into slices. I have seen
the kingdom deny its being the kingdom,
and now no one will believe me. There is a place
of hope there, even if most days I don't
even believe in it, in the kingdom, even if
each time it leaves in the morning. No apple
blossoms on the water each time she surfaced.
No fletchings made from turkey feathers.
No script for how gently to close the screen door.

Forecast

each year I want to but can't shed my bones watch
myself from any day other than the present there has to be
a way to lose this velvet all I wasn't in the mirror

I should be growing this unending rain clinking off
the tin roof into the drainpipes the weather said rain

for days last night I woke with pain changes
in the barometric pressure I felt in my joints
not wanting to inherit this inheriting it nonetheless

from my father asleep downstairs on the couch I want
to wake him and tell him all I dreamed about the deer

Prayer

O leafless branch O asphalt underneath
me O guardrail in your silver keep me safe
on the path O pinched nerve in my back O God
in the ductwork in every shingle of each
roof each house I pass O guardrail this road
is beat to shit and you know it too O crumpled
receipt in my pocket I don't remember what
I paid for but I just know I have O winter
the season my sister went without power cold
in her apartment her man curled into her keeping
her warm or just less cold O sister your picture
on the wall of our father's house looking out
at me to look back O memory lodged like an ice
pick in my head O guardrail keep me straight
on the path when I want to throw him against
the wall like he did her O clenched jaw I never had
courage when given the chance to end it I didn't
O flock of buzzards no longer circling just waiting
on the ground for their turn O buzzards pick my bones
clean let my ribs sing in the wind if the wind
so passes over them O blown-out candle
give me the finality of amen without having
to say it O dust let my bones forget
where they came from and where they are going

Worry Stone

as I grab one from the basket in the store   that round quartz stone
with a cross carved into it   I think of all the times my body
would not let me get off the floor   another panic attack   I called
my mother four states away   told her my goodbyes   it was the end
for me   I knew   the paramedics carried me from my apartment
to the ambulance where if only I had a worry stone   maybe I
could've held it in my palm until   the fear left my body a crumpled
mess   who among you   can add a single hour to his life
from worrying   the word of my Lord spoke   the siren in the air
I was alone with the Lord I was alone   the road pulled away
from me   through those two back windows like my future
unspooling   the streetlights getting smaller and full of shadows
until   my parents dropped me off   I was checking into
that hospital   the only reason I was let home each night because
I lied about being suicidal   said I needed a smoke   or some air
who wouldn't be   who wouldn't want   to kill themselves
when their chest became a stone   each arm   a stone   each arm
an extension of that carved cross   if I unclenched my hand
would the shape   of that stone   be imprinted on my palm
would I still be   in that apartment   looking down at my body
as if through the wrong end of a telescope   do not Paul wrote
be anxious   about anything   no prayer pulled me from this

76

one   or that one   there I was   bent on death as the best option

to stop the panic   the worry   my goddamn head   from opening

into the morning light   O Lord to be with you   I could

let go of the stone for once   and be free

Trusting the Periphery

here in my apartment boiling
   noodles on the stove, watching
      the water shimmer as it heats,
   the noodles dancing or doing
whatever it is that noodles do
   exactly,—but instead I'm looking out
      the side of my glasses, the periphery,
   what has happened between me
and her before the previous
   me and   her and   her and   her
      and her, worried that the pattern
   of instability I developed over
the steep hill of ten years will
   wreck what I try to hold still,
      here, in the kitchen, as she
   comes up behind me, puts her
arms through mine, and asks
   what time dinner will be ready.

Because Because

Because it wasn't exactly breaking and entering,
because it was your friend's house, because you knew
where they hid the key under the rock by the mailbox,
because you were supposed to feed their cats
while they were gone, because they were your friends
not mine, because when we fucked on their couch
we cleaned up after, because the heat was turned
almost completely off, because you were shivering naked
against the leather, because it wasn't exactly stealing
when I opened their bottle of Cordella nestled behind
the cat litter, because I knew we were both only home
for the holiday, because we were there almost
two hours before we remembered to even feed
the cats, because you smelled like cinnamon, because
I was trying my hardest not to add weight to our actions,
because now you were living on the other side of the country,
because when you tripped over the Christmas lights
I laughed, because it wasn't exactly drunk if you could
still walk a straight line on their hardwood floor,
because the worn grain felt smooth against my socks,
because your friend's cats needed feeding, we fed them.

What We Are Given

To cut down on the number of coyotes
on his property, your father would soak

two-inch squares of sponge in bacon grease,
then litter them along the red dirt road.

He told you how they would stick in the intestines
of the animal, starving them from the inside out,

until one day, *No more coyote.* You could relate.
Their pepper coat, their eyes already glassy.

He didn't have to watch them, so it was easier
for him to distance himself. This, his duty

to the land, its unplowed fields. How, even
then, you wanted to stray, but you were too

young. How even now, you can't cook bacon
in the kitchen of your one-bedroom apartment

without thinking *Maybe, this time, if I'm lucky,
it'll kill me, too.* Off the bed of his truck

he made you toss one, then another,
those little red and blue squares were

a death sentence for the next blind hunger
who came along, who took of the soft meal

laid out before them, who didn't know
what they were given until it was too late.

Egg Tooth

Any way you face me, you're still naked.
Tell me about your father, his drinking,

where he is now. Tell me why you don't talk
to him. Tell me more. What I thought

I knew was wrong. My egg tooth breaks through
the outer membrane, lets me breathe. Finally.

The grace that comes with honesty—
I've been here before. *I love you, too.*

But do you? Be honest. This is the first time
you've stayed the night. Every piece

you share becomes, somehow, more important.
The first details always are: your hands,

your scent, the hair stuck against your neck—
new as light. My egg tooth pushing through,

blue shell cracking enough for me to feel
the smoothness of your legs against mine.

Your body unfolds like a ballerina. This new world,
our world. The sharpness of the tooth splintering

what kept us apart, what protected us.

Pygmalion

When I can't have you, I have your idea. Your idea
in my bedside lamp, your idea in my coffee cup.

Your idea floating on my ceiling, the glow-in-the-dark
plastic stars, the firefly in my mind. You, somewhere

in the idea of you. I want the idea of you. I want you.
Your idea walking in through wooden saloon doors.

Your idea the bubble and the breath inside the bubble.
The nail in my tire that if left, fits so well it holds

the air in, the gold coin I can't spend, the hairpin chip
in my windshield that never fully fractures. Your idea the wet

oak leaves I rake into piles in the yard. Your idea
in every crosswalk laced with sunlight, across the street,

around the corner, on the balcony overlooking the pool,
the pew I fell asleep on. Your idea the black bear pawing

the old meat in the oil drum, who smelled me downwind.
The brass casing of every bullet I've never shot. The removed

lead, the crimped end, the sulfur of the powder all over your fur.
I have tried forgetting, but every door I close you open.

Snowstorm, Mid-January

To keep the trains running in the snow,
they lit the tracks on fire. The crew
doused them in kerosene in order
to repair the connections. After three days

of drinking, I wake up with a hangover
that doesn't go away. I can imagine being
on one of those trains, my future two lines
of fire in front of me, the sizzle of snow

pocketed around the steel tracks. I make
coffee again but nothing helps my head.
My therapist told me I shouldn't drink
on my meds, but the cut crystal decanter

is a form of magic to the light around it
promising something even a therapist
can't. O blesséd benzo, will you calm
the panic for just a minute? I need

an escape from this body, if only for
a night, if only for a drink, a dose.
Shoveled coal, steam engine, take me
into the mountains of a good drunk,

I can heal if I can see the track laid out
like the instructions on a prescription
bottle's stickered label, if only to see
the track, O pills, O drinks, be my match.

Cartoon

Two hundred frames in, you decide the sketches
        are too shaky once set in motion. You throw them
                in the garbage, dump your spaghetti on top so
        there would be no way to salvage them. This repeats
again, except the second time with a filter of
        wet coffee grounds. Trace paper on top of trace
                paper on top of light board—you decide that in
        order to finish by morning, you'll have to
shorten the story. Yes, that's it. You'll skip the part
        where the bag of flour walks into the party
                full of other bags of flour. There, the jock.
        There, the princess. There, the wallflower. There,
the group of bags serving only as backdrop. You'll
        shorten the story because there isn't time
                to show this bag all alone, no other bags talking
        to him. There's not time to develop out this bag
of flour's character. Let's call him Harry. So you
        jump to the scene in the kitchen, in the room next
                to the party. You jump to where Harry cuts himself
        open with a steak knife, white powder spilling out all
over the linoleum floor. Harry doesn't bleed out long
        before you sketch him scooping himself up into
                a pan, pouring milk, raw eggs, sugar on top
        of himself. You jump to the scene where Harry puts
himself into the oven, the part where the other bags
        of flour smell something they don't recognize at first,
                where they walk into the kitchen, see
        an empty bag and a cake on the counter
with a note that says *I made this for you.*

Outpatient

For a short time, days at most, fawns
don't recognize predators or danger—
and I walked right up to one of them, held

the bleating thing in my arms. The creature
seemed of another time, and here I was,
a stranger in its sanctuary. Its ear already

tagged with a number, its tiny heart beating
twice as fast as mine, its white-spotted coat,
still new. I was coming off a new medicine,

or maybe I was starting another, so most things
only felt half-real. But its shallow breathing
wasn't a hallucination. Its eyes didn't know

what to do with mine yet. I was on leave
for the afternoon, halfway through the week
of Moving Forward, the mental hospital

program back home. After a few minutes
the fawn started to kick, the other deer
all looking at me, the outsider, as if I was

causing the small sounds of pain—
I the oncoming headlights, I the rifle barrel,
I the bear trap or bluetongue. The fawn kicked

until it was out of my arms, struggling
at first under its new weight, its legs
no thicker than my wrists. It ran toward

the trees, the other deer, its mother. I stood up
from the plastic chair. My chest was still
warm from where the animal had once been.

Notes

The epigraph of the book by Emily Dickinson is from Letter 261 [Thank You for the Surgery], written to T. W. Higginson. "Cain" borrows wording from Genesis 4:6 and John 8:7. "Watching My Father Pray over the Lord's Supper" borrows wording from Luke 22:19–20. "Worry Stone" borrows wording from Matthew 6:27 and Philippians 4:6.

Acknowledgments

Grateful acknowledgment to the editors of the following journals, where these poems (or versions of these poems) first appeared: *The Adriot Journal* "Fig Leaf," *The Baltimore Review* "Egg Tooth," *Barrow Street* "Carving," *Bayou Magazine* "My Father Feeding the Birds" (appeared as "Birds"), *Botticelli Magazine* "Outpatient," *The Cincinnati Review* "Prayer," *Diode* "When My Father Calls Me a Pussy," *Horsethief* "Pygmalion," *H.O.W. Journal* "Sour Wine," *Indiana Review* "Love Song to the Demon-Possessed Pigs of Gadara," *The Minnesota Review* "Nocturne with Choking in Calloway Gardens," *New England Review* "Aquarium" and "Birthmark," *New Ohio Review* "Tightrope," *New Orleans Review* "Cartoon," *New World Writing* "Because Because" and "Polar Bear," *Pleiades* "When You Were out of Town Last Weekend," *Poet Lore* "Floodwaters in South Carolina," *Poetry Northwest* "There Is No Power in Blame," *Prairie Schooner* "Ash on the Tongue," *Rattle* "Images of Kurt Cobain's Shotgun Released," "Upon Receiving My Inheritance," and "Ode to the Mattress on the Side of the Interstate," *Salt Hill* "Elegy with Digital Flowers," *The Threepenny Review* "Not an Entrance," *Tinderbox Poetry Review* "Forecast," *Valparaiso Poetry Review* "What We Are Given," *Washington Square Review* "Porcelain Nocturne."

The poem "Sugar" was originally published by the Academy of American Poets on their website Poets.org. "Song" and "Emo, 2005" originally appeared in *Narrative* magazine.

Also, many thanks to the following people for their help with this manuscript: James Kimbrell, Virgil Suárez, David Kirby, Barbara Hamby, Andrew Epstein, Juan Carlos Galeano, Joshua Weiner,

Stanley Plumly, Elizabeth Arnold, Michael Collier, M.K. Foster, FM Stringer, Rita Mookerjee, Rob Stephens, Paige Lewis, Dustin Pearson, Tanya Grae, Marianne Chan, Linda Gregerson, Peter Campion, Brenda Shaughnessy, James McCoy, everyone at the University of Iowa Press, and forever, Molly Marotta.

Iowa Poetry Prize
and Edwin Ford Piper Poetry Award Winners

1987
Elton Glaser, *Tropical Depressions*
Michael Pettit, *Cardinal Points*

1988
Bill Knott, *Outremer*
Mary Ruefle, *The Adamant*

1989
Conrad Hilberry, *Sorting the Smoke*
Terese Svoboda, *Laughing Africa*

1990
Philip Dacey, *Night Shift at the Crucifix Factory*
Lynda Hull, *Star Ledger*

1991
Greg Pape, *Sunflower Facing the Sun*
Walter Pavlich, *Running near the End of the World*

1992
Lola Haskins, *Hunger*
Katherine Soniat, *A Shared Life*

1993
Tom Andrews, *The Hemophiliac's Motorcycle*
Michael Heffernan, *Love's Answer*
John Wood, *In Primary Light*

1994
James McKean, *Tree of Heaven*
Bin Ramke, *Massacre of the Innocents*
Ed Roberson, *Voices Cast Out to Talk Us In*

1995
Ralph Burns, *Swamp Candles*
Maureen Seaton, *Furious Cooking*

1996
Pamela Alexander, *Inland*
Gary Gildner, *The Bunker in the Parsley Fields*
John Wood, *The Gates of the Elect Kingdom*

1997
Brendan Galvin, *Hotel Malabar*
Leslie Ullman, *Slow Work through Sand*

1998
Kathleen Peirce, *The Oval Hour*
Bin Ramke, *Wake*
Cole Swensen, *Try*

1999
Larissa Szporluk, *Isolato*
Liz Waldner, *A Point Is That Which Has No Part*

2000
Mary Leader, *The Penultimate Suitor*

2001
Joanna Goodman, *Trace of One*
Karen Volkman, *Spar*

2002
Lesle Lewis, *Small Boat*
Peter Jay Shippy, *Thieves' Latin*

2003
Michele Glazer, *Aggregate of Disturbances*
Dainis Hazners, *(some of) The Adventures of Carlyle, My Imaginary
    Friend*

2004
Megan Johnson, *The Waiting*
Susan Wheeler, *Ledger*

2005
Emily Rosko, *Raw Goods Inventory*
Joshua Marie Wilkinson, *Lug Your Careless Body out of the Careful Dusk*

2006
Elizabeth Hughey, *Sunday Houses the Sunday House*
Sarah Vap, *American Spikenard*

2008
Andrew Michael Roberts, *something has to happen next*
Zach Savich, *Full Catastrophe Living*

2009
Samuel Amadon, *Like a Sea*
Molly Brodak, *A Little Middle of the Night*

2010
Julie Hanson, *Unbeknownst*
L. S. Klatt, *Cloud of Ink*

2011
Joseph Campana, *Natural Selections*
Kerri Webster, *Grand & Arsenal*

2012
Stephanie Pippin, *The Messenger*

2013
Eric Linsker, *La Far*
Alexandria Peary, *Control Bird Alt Delete*

2014
JoEllen Kwiatek, *[Study for Necessity]*

2015
John Blair, *Playful Song Called Beautiful*
Lindsay Tigue, *System of Ghosts*

2016
Adam Giannelli, *Tremulous Hinge*
Timothy Daniel Welch, *Odd Bloom Seen from Space*

2017
Alicia Mountain, *High Ground Coward*
Lisa Wells, *The Fix*

2018
Rob Schlegel, *88 Trees*
Cassie Donish, *The Year of the Femme*

2019
William Fargason, *Love Song to the Demon-Possessed Pigs of Gadara*
Jennifer Habel, *The Book of Jane*